J. J. Harkins

Lord Attenborough's only Son, and Katie Jurose, the Abducted Girl

J. J. Harkins

Lord Attenborough's only Son, and Katie Jurose, the Abducted Girl

ISBN/EAN: 9783337420154

Printed in Europe, USA, Canada, Australia, Japan

Cover: Foto ©ninafisch / pixelio.de

More available books at **www.hansebooks.com**

ACT I.

Scene First. The inside of Lord Attenborough's house, with a view of a Park in rear, and a Castle in the distance.

Enter Lord Attenborough and Lady, who take seats on right of room.

Lord A.—Ha, ha, ha! I observe our villagers are in holiday glee to-day. But this is over, perhaps, some future expectation.

Lady A.—It is well for them to have a day from the toils of the field, but it might also be well to bridle their felicity.

Lord A.—O! my dear Lady.——

Enter Cyrus through the left door.

Cyrus—My Lord, the village is alive with excitement in anticipation of the marriage of Sir Reuben, your son and their benefactor.

Lady A.—[rising.]—Pray tell me to whom is my son going to be married, and from whom did you get the information?

Cyrus.—The informant positively refused to throw any more light upon it, but recent events have convinced me that she is his father's servant, Katie.

Lady A.—Well, well! this is enough to break down even the most constant. This is astounding. I thought something unnatural was about to befall me. Now I am convinced by a sad realization of the fact.—the servant of his father for a wife. Did I ever think my only son would betake himself to such a den of vice and poverty as this?

Lord A.—Many, many a bright, unsullied soul dwells in these poor hovels, or imaginary dens of vice and poverty, notwithstanding the manner in which they may be represented to us. I held views similar to yourself, (placing his hand on her shoulder,) and in my denunciation I told him the reward for his conduct in acting without his parents consent, would bring upon him confusion and neglect. I also told him he would merit the displeasure of yourself and me for ever. But, subsequent events induced me to be more lenient.

Lady A.—So he has his father's approval of his choice? Well, he has not, or will not have his mother's. I will infringe upon the right granted him in this case, by using every effort in my power to check this rash of his. I am entrusted with his welfare through all the vicissitudes of life and must save him from the life of an everlasting minion. Reflect for a moment of the disgrace it will bring upon yourself and your noble ancestors. I see that I am now called upon to exercise an instrument which I never had occasion to use before. It is necessary that I should stay a design which, if carried out, must prove disastrous to our general happiness.

Lord A.—We should endeavor to be reconciled with his choice. You remember well the days of our own courtship. Although our families were of equal rank, no barrier, however strong, could stay that love, which I hope, will carry us down into old age, and which we know is infinitely nobler than wealth or fame.

Lady A.—Your generous language will fall very short of exciting any sympathy in me. That would have been pleasant food for meditation many years ago. Now it is, to me, all a fiction. I dare say had you borne the pressure of his future happiness as keenly as I do, you would not barter away, into the hands of ruffians, your whole domain, which should come to him as it came to you. We must insist upon tearing asunder the engagement; and also, we should insist upon her removal from this house. By virtue of my maternal authority, Miss Hulda was to be his bride. She is a lady of culture and good parents, if not wealthy. Yes, one who, I think, will be more suitable to a Knight of his ability. Alas! did I ever think the friendship with Katie would ripen into love.

Lord A.—As to her removal from this house, it is useless. Love is not lost with sight nor does it gain its height in an instant Love, a rosy-cheeked child, is likened to Sol, the great centre of the solar system. When seen in the eastern skies he is, to us, mild and timid, but at the approach of noon-day the intensity of his-heat becomes sometimes unbearable. And, although gradually sinking below the western horizon, we should remember that he loses not one shadow of his lustre. So it is with love. At first approach it is timid, but as time passes away, it grows warmer and warmer, till the summit is gained, which is a permanent union. You may cause a separation, but, like the sun going into his hiding place, he only goes to return another day, perhaps more brilliant than before. I therefore exhort you to let prudence be your guide.

Lady A.—O mercy! thus does my every project meet with disapprobation or inadvertance! To whom shall I now go for consolation? I will go into seclusion and remain there forever. [Exit Lady A. through l. d.]

Lord A.—[Solus.]—In congruence with my wife's desire, and for the maintainence of harmony in my house, I would do anything in my power, but to the persecution of a poor girl I cannot and will not consent.

Enter Cyrus through L. D.

Cyrus.—My Lord, two officers of peace are at in the shrubbery of the Park and demand admission to the Castle, at the same time saying that some miscreant has secreted himself within the circuit of its limit.

Lord A.—Go put them to flight. Disperse them. Do they think my house is Goal for villians ? [Exit Cyrus through l. d.]

Lord A. - [Solus.]—When Pride, the father of all evil and the enemy of mankind, fills the human heart with an over zeal in any cause, it destroys the noblest virtue, charity ; and leads its victim up the hill of fame to the very summit of its ambition. But in accordance with the old proverb, "after pride comes a fall," the unfortunate is often ignominously hurried down the precipice of despair, there to meet with the sneers and rebukes of the multitude.

Enter Cyrus through L. D.

Cyrus.—My Lord it is extremely necessary that you should make a personal visit to the spot to prevent their doing mischief, as they are becoming boisterous and refuse to be dispersed.

Lord A.—Rascals, what do they mean ?

[Exit Lord A. through l. d.]

[Cyrus remains in the room.]

Cyrus.—[nerveously,] [pulling his coat about him.]—Having disposed of his Lordship I will serve my mistress in the capacity of an officer of the peace.

[Cyrus then goes to r. d. and admits the two abductors.]

Cyrus.—Now that you have gained an entrance it is essentially important that you should know the way to take your charge without the interference of the old Seneschal, who may stop you if he sees you, and who is to be walking about the Park.

Ralph.—[Gruffly.]—We 'ill waste no time with her. She better—

Cyrus.—Hush, hush! Know you not that the Lord of this domain is, perhaps, within hearing distance of us?

Seba.—[Timidly.]—We better have nothing to do with this poor girl.

Ralph.—Ain't we go'en to 'get the bricks for it? I'll have somth'en to do with you directly.

Cyrus.—[Nerveously.]—Come now, for mercy sake do not disappoint me at this critical moment.

Ralph.—You gimme the girl, and I'll fix him if he don't help.

Cyrus.—The work must be done in an artistic manner, and with as much haste as possible. I will wear a mask, so that in the event of her ever turning up again she cannot recognize me as her abductor.

Ralph.—I'll keep her where she 'll not recognize you, I'll bet.

Cyrus.—Cross the culvert in the Park, down the lane, through that little woods at the foot of the hill, and over the torrent. Follow out my plan and your escape is certain.

Cyrus.—[Then takes them to her apartment, and they bandage her mouth. She is then taken across the room by Cy., Ral. and Seb. Exit through r. d.]

Enter Cyrus in a great hurry, takes off his mask and readjusts his garments.

Enter Lady A. through l. d.

Lady A.—All is consummate.

Enter Lord A. through l. d.

Lord A.—[Rubbing his hands.]—Ha, ha, ha! the rascals were unanimous in their opinion for once, I presume. But they generally do be in such cases.

Cyrus.—Yes, my Lord, I saw them fly in dismay at your approach.

Lord A.—[Handing him a note.]—Give this to the footman, tell him to deliver it into hands of the goaler forthwith.

Exit Cyrus through l. d.

Lord A.—[mirthfully.]—My dear lady, you have ostensibly recovered from the effect of your little embarassment. Still, I venture to say your turbulent spirit will only be satisfied with the consummation of some mischief.

Lady A.—[nervously.]—No, but on the contrary I have given my consent and become reconciled by applying your kind words as a salve to the wounds which I received upon the first announcement of the event; I have chosen to be her friend and protectress, rather than an enemy.

Lord A.—I am happy to hear you say it. It is in accord with the finer teaching of humanity. Burnish a mirror and it will smile back with an increased lustre. So it is with a kind word to the lowly, it will be a source of consolation, even ih the shadows of the darkest hours of life. Come, let us have a stroll in the Park? [Exit Lord A. and Lady A. through l. d.]

Cyrus.—I wish that inhuman old footman would return with an answer, an excuse or something. I suppose he has fallen asleep on the way.

[Enter Tim. through R. D., holding his leg.]

Cyrus.—How in the mischief did you get in here?

Tim.—I clum over the fence. O ha! I'll nivir do it ag'in; [in an undertone,] that divil owa dug.

Cyrus.—Vagabond, never come here again in that way. That is the entrance for distinguished visitors and friends of the family

Tim.—Over the fence. Be dad, [catching his leg,] if they all meet the same reception that I did, they paid dear for their friendship.

Cyrus.—Who is that old scoundrel that is with you?

Tim.—The messenger sid to send-ush-all, and we all went.

Cyrus.—Begone from here immediately. If his Lordship knew what you were he would send for the robbers, to the exclusion of you and your illustrious followers.

Tim.—Sure and I only did phat ye tould me to do.

Cyrus.—Did he tell you to climb over a mountain of a wall to gain access to Lord Attenborough's mansion? Did he tell you to walk right in without admission from any one?

Tim.—Well, what do you want wid me?

Cyrus.—I do not want you. Go to Seneschal.

Tim.—[To himself]—Send-ush-all, send-ush-all, what way will I go this time?

Cyrus.—Come with me, I will show you an aperture through which you can get away. [Exit Cyrus and Tim. through l. d.]

Enter Lady A. through C. D., with clasped hands.

Lady A.—[Solus.]—I perceive this is the time of visitation. Like the raging storms over a restless sea do my timely admon- itions assail my guilty conscience! O Heavenly powers assist me to bear the bitter anguish that now penetrates my very soul in the solitude of the future! The child whom I loved and cherished till old age hath clothed my head in a garment of white has left his home, his kindred and his native land for the wilds of an unknown clime, there to live out an existence, untold of, perhaps unheard of.

Enter Lord A. through C. D.

Lord A.—My dear lady your walk was short, and, I presume, void of all pleasure. What has destroyed that peace which outlined your beautiful countenance but such a short time ago? Perphaps [placing his hand on her shoulder,] the chilllng air is too depressing upon you? Without your presence the Park is, to me, like the barren desert. How cold. Pray tell me what your motives are for this behavior? Have I given offense, in any way, if so tell me in what manner? I will rectify any wrong that may have been done, at the cost of my whole estate.

Lady A.—[gravely,] You have done me no harm. Your good heart and kind words have always been like that of a noble husand and a loving father. You are willing, I know to sacrifice your whole estate for me. But my trouble is of a nature that requires no sacrifices at all ; all the sacrifice is made.

Lord A.—Ah! [gravely,] be as reluctant as possible. I fear something more than ordinary is coming. Something to bring remorse and discontent into our once happy home. But tell me, that I may condole with you.

Lady A.—The tortures of your lasting words upon me,with the loss of an only son is our future trouble. [She sinks into the chair broken down.]

ACT FIRST. SCENE SECOND.

[The inside of a barn-like house, with three old chairs and table. Katie sitting in the corner.]

Enter Mother through a side gate.

Mother.– Yes, she is sick again. Such a lazy hulk of a girl I never saw. Come over here, [gruffly,] and help me to move this table about little. When I was your age I had to work like an ox. The boys will be in directly for dinner, and I will see if they have hired a lady to loaf around here, and their poor old mother to kill herself for them. I tell you to come on now and give your poor old mother a help.

Enter Ralph and Seba through side gate.

Ral.—Well, lazy, sick again? Born sick, I reckon? Oh! won't speak, won't you? Come here, move 'round, will you? You won't be here long 'afore I learn you how to work, you lazy hulk. [Giving her a push across the floor.] Mother, git my dinner ready, will you?

Mother.—I just want to know if you boys has hired that lazy girl for a lady. It's a shame that your poor old mother has to go around working like a slave of Siberia,

Seb.—It's cruilty in the shape of correction.

Ral.—Listen to old honey-suckle. You are as bad as she is.

Seb.—I am only taking the side of a poor, innocent, helpless girl against ruffians.

Ral.—What ! you gurilla. The next time you say that will be your last.

Seb.—No man who claims to have a spark of manhood in his body would abuse a girl without friends.

Ral.—What! do you mean to call me a coward by your double mean'en words you pupet ? Git out of my sight, or I will pitch you over the wall.

Mother.—He is good natured where he shoulden't be. If he

had to struggle about here like his poor old mother does in her old age, he'd know how to deal with every old tramp that comes around.   •

Seb.—[aside,] Poor creature, if she is compelled to remain here her lot will certainly be a sad one. I regret, when too late, that I ever became a party to such a base scheme as this. Here she is sick from fright, and apparently unconscious of the cuffs and abuses that await her. There will be a day of rectitude for all this. The Lord of Hosts certainly sees this work with a keen eye.

- Ral.—[walking over.] Well old woman, are you meditating on something sublime, or may I ask you what? [Stooping gently. Turning to Katie.] Well, lazy, I am go'en out now. Perhaps you will find your tongue by the time I come back?

[Exist Ral. through side gate.]

Mother.—If you had married my son you would have had a good home and a kind mother.

Katie.—O mercy! How could I marry such a man as that? Heaven guard me against such a rash act. A man from whom I received little less than the tortures of death.

Mother.—What! you udent marry my poor son? You rascal.

[Exit.]

Seb.--[walking over to Katie.] I am happy to see that you are recovering from the shock of your fright. Be cheerful; it is hard that is so, but by being patient you will make good your escape. Should everything else fail, I have devised a plan by which your return home is sure.

Katie.—O! for pity sake, please tell me before he comes back again. And should the wild beasts of the forest devour me in my journey I will risk it.

Seb.—The plan is this : Retire to-night as usual, and with as much complacency as possible. When at midnight, through the instrumentality of a friend, the village bells, some distance off, will be rung, which will immediately bring him to the scene of conflagration. Then I will take a board from the top of the house and lay it from eaves of the shanty to the wall, so that you can walk across and off. [Enter Ral. unnoticed.]

Katie.—Do ; I implore you to use every plan as tacitly as possible. Assist me to return to my home, to my aged mother, her to whom I owe my support, and may the intermineable glory that awaits the just be your reward. May He, to whom all the mysteries of nature belong, strengthen you. And, again, may He whom the Heavens and the earth cannot contain, bless and guide you safely through all the vicissitudes of life. This I give you from the fullness of a grateful heart.

Seb.—Be assured that I, under every and all circumstances, will be your friend, no matter how trying they may be.

Katie.—Thank you. You have been the only source of comfort I had since the time of my abduction. I wonder that a heart so generous as yours could dwell in such a wilderness of ignorance iniquity.

Ral.—[making himself visible.]—You will take a board off the roof, will you ? [Catches Seb. and throws him across the room.] and gives her a slight push. I will attend to the roof and you, too. [Katie noticed to be weeping.]

Seb.—I must put up with your cuffs and abuses, I suppose. But I will not see this poor girl knocked around any more. I will give you all I am worth. [Struggle ensues in which Seba is worsted.]

    Enter Mother.

Mother.—Ralph, what's your brother doing?

Ral.—He's laying plans for herto git away.

Mother.—That's right, give it to 'em then.

Seb.—Yes, you encourage him, for fear his brutality is not at a high enough pitch now.

Mother.—Well, you should be like a Christian, and do what your poor good mother tells you to do. I'm sure I struggle hard enough to raise you both and make you smart.

Ral.—You intend to show fight again, do you? It's well for you that your mother is here, or I would give you something to carry all the days of your life. And as for her; well, she's got to stay here all the days of her life. Any man that 'ill go back on his brother and mother is'nt worthy to be called a man. I tell you if you help her to get away from here, well, for that offense you must die; and should her village friends find out where she is and force in upon us, you must bear the brunt of it as well as me. And you, lazy, I am determined that your thoughts will be more of an earthly nature by keeping your hands at work.

Katie.—[timidly.]—It's to be supposed that I must submit to that or anything else your Lordship sees fit to impose upon me; it is only one of a whole series of tortures which I have been compelled to endure under your unbearable tyranny. But [turning aside] how can I hope for any redress for my wrongs here, since those in whom I placed my trust have abandoned me in my utmost need?

Ral.—Do you hear the talk of her? She cu'm down from the

clouds. She must have been learning how to talk from some Lord. Well, it's nice to hear her chirp anyhow.

Mother.—Yes, she can learn a body how to talk, but she can't learn you how to work.

Ral.—[gruffly,] Go out to the pit and git my ax. I don't want any moaning about, either.

[Exit Katie through side gate. Lightning is seen in the darkness, and rain falls heavily.]

Mother.—She 'ill get away from us, I tell you, Ralph, I'll go out and watch 'er. [Exit.]

Ral.—I am not afearn of her gite'n away.

Enter Katie with ax.

Ral.—Now sharp it while you are able. We 'll have to take 'er to the burying ground the first place. [To Katie.] Say, lazy, if you don't want to forget how to talk you better say somethin'. Won't answer, won't you ?

Seb.—[in low tone.] You are one of the meauest of men.

Ral.—Well, grumbler, I hear a moan from your corner. What's trouble over there? Your mamma's gone out, maybe tha's what's wrong with you. She 'ill be in directly, I reckon. I am afeard to go out fear you'd take a board off the roof. You may take it off when I'm here, but you must learn how to walk over me first, and you was'nt born to do that.

Enter Mother, in a hurry.

Mother.—[excitedly.]—Ralph, Ralph, an armed body of men's scoutin' the woods for this hulk of a girl. Put her out; hurry, put her out. [Sensation.]

Ral.—Bolt the door, quick.

Mother.—They'll kill the man that has her. I always tried to be kind and motherly to her,

Ral.—I was'nt, and never will be. Let them come. I'll take it for the best and look for the worst. The man that breaks open that door must suffer the penalty, which is nothing short of his life. Make ready there, granny, to fight the battle. Every man should fight for the protection of his home.

Seb.—Your time is well nigh run. I have been your friend and accomplice in all the diabolical acts which you have committed in these woods, but you, by your brutality to that poor, lone girl have revealed to me the light of a new life.

Ral.—Ay, then, you'r not go'en to help me if they find us. You are as bad as me, and you must bear the result of your work too.

Seb.—If I must suffer, it will not be in defense of your cruelty.

Ral.—Ah, lad, you might as well die game as die like a deserter. [Loud noise heard from the outside. Cries of here she is, here she is.]

The door is burst open. Enter William.

Bill.—O Katie! bless your dear little heart I thought I'd see your face again. How are you anyhow? Which of these is the man who took you from your poor old mother. [Kate points out Ralph.]

Bill—Villain what right had you to take this girl away from her home?

Ral.—I had the right that allows a man to break into my house witout my permission. I have another right [pulling out a large knife] which is the common right of every man in this country.

Bill.—I will contest your right to do such tricks as this for the future. If your fashion of doing things meets with success, then it is not my fault.

Ral.—I tell you to git out or your life's not worth the time it'll take to give it flight. The man was never knowen about this country to enter Ralph Browe's shanty without the loss of his life· Curse the impudence of the man [preparing for the final struggle] that burst the door of my shanty. Should this act of cowardice of mine find it's way through the surrouding country on me I am done for. You must pay for—[Rushes at Bill in a rage, but before he has time to use his weapon Seb. springs on his back and tightly holds his arms, while Bill. takes his knife and is about to deal him a blow, but suddenly throwing up hi arms he says: "Ah! villain your life belongs to me. Will you beg for mercy.

Ral.—There beats a heart within my bosom that was never knowen to yield to any man. So plunge your cursed steel as I would. As for mercy I know it not.

Bill.—[Throwing the weapon down] My heart fails me; I know you deserve it but I cannot.

·ACT FIRST, SCENE THIRD.

[The outside of Sir Henry Rollin's house and a portion of the Park with fence and gate on the right. On the left hand a tree with a rustic seat beneath it.

Enter Sir Reuben from Park.

Reuben [Solus] Ah me! are my senses right or am I only enjoying the sweet visions of childhood's slumber? Many years ago I spent the delights of my youth in yonder Mansion. There I received all the fondness and tenderness that could emanate from

a Mother's heart. But alas! a change came, I loved, for which I paid the severest penalty. Yes I incurred upon myself the heaviest denunciation from one whom, to me, anything else but love seemed at variance with human nature. And during this period of time I've not had the pleasure to behold for once the countenance of the one for whom I have undergone all the hardships and privations to which unsettled man is subjected to. Well it takes all such things, perhaps, to make up an eventful life. [Looking anxiously] The administrator of my father's estate made an appointment to meet me here at noon, in consequence of which I must while the time as well as I can.
[He takes the rustic seat under the tree.]

     Enter Admr.

Admr.— Happy to meet you this morning. [Shaking hands.]

Sir Reuben—Hearing of the demise of my parents and knowing myself to be the only heir to their vast domain, I deemed it highly prudent to investigate all the peculiar circumstances connected with it and if possible, to reinstate myself in the old domicile. For this object have I traveled from the remotest part of · Christiandom.

Admr.—Your parents' will is in perfect accord with your cause. Your mother repented bitterly of her hasty action, and your good old father confident of his son's returning home some day, left his whole domain in readiness for that end. But that is not all: the general belief that you are dead (caused by your mysterious disappearnce and long absence) has been confirmed by the lady now occupying your father's house. "She and you," so the story runs, "were married and lived happily together, as all newly married couples do live, when suddenly you became dizzied with the flattering words of other women and forgetful of your nuptial promises, abandoned her. But she, aftter the elapse of considerable time, fully convinced of your uuhappy fate married again." Her husband is a man, haughty and if necessary desperate. Knowing as I do his character and the result that must follow a reverse of this kind, I almost dread the undertaking.

Sir Reuben—May I advance a plan by which your person will be free from danger?

Admr.—It would be very appropriate under the present circumstances, though I see no way to avoid it.

Sir Reuben—Yes, here is a plan, meet the man before nightfall; tell him confidentially that you have left the necessary documents with the rightful heir, which will naturally cause the channel of his vengeance to flow upon me, for be it understood that, should the hazard of a life be necesssary, *or any other contingency*, my desire is that I should bear it.

Admr.—To say nothing of your courage, I admire the extremes to which you would resort for my personal safety. But, would it not be in the highest degree deplorable in me to desert the executive duties that I so faithfully promised to carry out to the best of my ability? However, it may be necessary to divert his mind, you may avail yourself of this opportuuity to meet him I will let you carry out your plan and await future developments.

[Exit Admr. gives him papers]

Sir Reu.—[Solus] Now it might be fitting to search the one for whom my heart has yearned so long.

Enter Kate unnoticed and takes seat under tree.

Kate—Lul, lul, lul, lah! [Dolefully]

Sir Reu.—[Looking anxiously] Ah! by the sparkle of her eye,

that is she now. Or perhaps it is some Etherial foci that I see, a hidden treasure which is again only to fade away. (approaching,) May I intrude upon your kindness by requesting your name and from whence you came?

Kate.—(Reluctantly) My name is Katie Durose.

Sir Reu.—(Anxiously) Katie Durose? Katie Durose?

Katie.—Yes, sir.

Sir. Reu.—(with a sigh.)—Ah! I thought it was. May I ask where your present home is?

Katie—In yonder Mansion. (moving away.)

Sir. Reu.—(Suddenly) back again to the old domicle? Do you ever expect to meet again the friend you once had in yonder Mansion?

Katie.—(Cheering up) O! I would be so rejoiced to see him once again, but (saddening) I fear I never shall.

Sir. Reu.—(handing her a letter) This may remind you of things come and gone. This is the last one I ever had the pleasure to receive from you.

Katie —(Astonished) From me! Is it possible that you arc Reuben Attenborough?

Reu.—You have said it right (They embrace.)

Katie.—This brings back to me those happy days with so many pleasant recollections, that I almost wish they had never passed.

Sir Reu.—I assure you my heart never forgot you. I was about to search every nook and corner in the whole village for you, and were I to gain my former standing, renew if possible the old friendship which, I presume, is not dead but only sleeping.

Katie.—Should the elements that prompted me to love you grow cold and lifeless from the fact of your slight embarrassment or at the approach of poverty, they would be but a mockery and unworthy of the name. No, the motives that prompted you to sacrifice so much are too rare a jewel to pass without a recompense.

Sir Reu.—Ah! then I may well conclude that the old love, which slept so long, is still there with all that innocent grandeur which so often indelibly stamps the countenance of the virtuous.

Katie.—You well know it.

Reu.—Ah well! I don't regret all that I may have gone through for you, for it was a worthy object. You shouldn't have spoken; your actions told me.

Katie.—O happy spot, yet it cost many tears.

Sir Reu.—But was not the cause a good one?

Katie.—Ah was it. I mingled my sorrow with yours because I knew or believed you must have met with a sad end.

Sir. Reu.—Though kind Providence preserved my life, you may well suppose that my cast was a hard one. Still knowing the meaning of your last words as I did my consoling hope of another happy meeting was of the most assuring nature. When I say another happy meeeting I mean the one that lasts forever

Katie.—Did you not think that, forgetting my promise, I I might marry another?

Sir Reu.—The thought never crossed my mind. [taking her hands] Having to fill a engagement which I just made previous to our meeting a brief leave of absence must be. Farewell.

[Exit Sir Rueben through l. s.]

Enter Bill from right.

Bill.—[with enthusiam] O Katie, how glad I am to see you again!

Katie.—[gladly] Dear cousin Bill, guess who came back to the village.

Bill.—Who?

Katie—Sir Reuben Attenborough, he who left his home so long ago. O do you mind the good old times he, you and I used to have jumping fences, climbing trees and leaping ditches? Do you mind how we used to watch the big wheel at the grist-mill r–r–r–r–r–r–r and how we used to splash to water to get the miller to race us.

Bill.—[seriously] Yes. I'll never forget the last splashing. He caught me the day after it. You did the splashing and he caught me for it. But when did he come back?

Katie.—The dear fellow; only a couple of days ago. I call him fellow because I am so familiar with him.

Bill.—You'r getin' so particular about your talking, that I can't have the good old time fun we us't to have. Them days you us't to say him and me.

Katie.—[seriously] O yes Bill. I am always your cousin and friend anyhow.

Bill.—Ha ha ha; that will be another holiday for us anyhow. We 'ort to have the old donkey agin.

Katie—[in an undertone] What did you do with that old donkey you used to try to ride?

Bill.—You was right that time. [with an air of triumph.]

Katie.—Why?

Bill.—Well we could never ride him.

Katie—Well what did you do with him? The poor old creature.

Bill—[seriously] Well we started to back one day; and

he backed; and he backed till he backed under the mill-wheel.

Katie—Poor old thing we used to have more fun trying to ride him. I am so sorry.

Bill—O that's nothing all our family was that way; our family don't notice that much.

Katie—Ha, ha, ha, he, he, he!

Bill—Katie sing me one of them songs you ust' to sing us in the meadows after harvest time.

Katie—[snickering and laughing.] Can't Bill.

Blll— Why? [looking in her face]

Katie—Had no business to back that donkey under the wheel so you had'nt.

Bill—Ha, ha, ha, ha, crying about the donkey.

Song by Katie.

Katie—What did you do with the turkey gobbler that aunt used to have?

Bill—It's up there yet.

Katie—I would have gone up there many a time had it not been for that old thing. Last time I went out there it raced me all over the cornfields.

Bill—We'r goin to have a raisin' out there to-morrow, and if you come I'll tell Liz so that she can have her gingham suit done up in time.

Katie—Poor Liz. I thought that you would have married her long before this time. You mind the day you kissed her, aha! You thought we did'nt see you. You don't mind that? I intend to tell aunt the very next time I go up.

Bill—That was the day she fainted. That didn't make her faint. She fell and hurt her foot.

Katie—[emphatically] No wonder. O ! do you mind the feet?

Bill—[bashfully] I never looked at her feet.

Katie—They were ponderous. If she wasn't a big strong girl she couldn't carry them.

Bill—Come out to-morrow with me and you and Liz shall have a hunkey time. [bouncing around.

[Cyrus comes from the house and catches him jumping about.]

Cy.—Have you nothing else to do except lounging about with every old beggar that comes within the limits of the village ?

Katie—[timidly] This is my cousin.

Cy.—I don't care who he is. Your Mistress needs you.

[Exit Katie in the house and Bill through the park.]

En'er Sir Henry Rollins.

Sir Hen.—[angrily] Some measure conducive to tranquility must be taken forthwith. [saddening] But, Alas! to check the villains in their design to deprive me of my estate, is something with which I am done.

Cy.—The audacity of the scoundrel is startling.

Sir Hen.—Sure I am told that he is but a mere inventive genius who, in conjunction with an alleged administrator, has devised a plan by which they can depose of me and gain a prize.

Enter Administrator, whose presence is ignored by Sir Henry.

Amr.—Happy morning. I came expressly to inform you that by the urgent request of my client, I have entirely given up the prosecution of this case.

Sir Hen.—You made a serious mistake by starting it. What have you done with the alleged documents you held ?

Admr.—Believing him to be the only son of the late Lord At-

tenborough and the rightful heir to his father's estate I delivered
all the necessary papers into his hands.

Sir Hen.—Be consistent for once in this preverse attitude
which you have taken and give me those documents to the exclusion of that inveterate villain with whom you have united
yourself to accomplish my ruin; give them I say for your life's
sake.

Admr.—Believe me the papers are with the owner.

Sir Hen.—[looking carefully around] Give me those papers
or, by hell and vengeance I will be a rut in which the wheels of
your life shall stick fast.

Admr.—Ah! the risk is your own I am not to be deterred
from the sense of right by your threats or entreaties. I must ex-
ecute faithfully to the best of my ability the duties imposed upon
me by his worthy parents, which I did by transmitting to him his
father's will·

Sir Hen.—[excitedly] Whose parents? Utter that word no
more. You have presumed to much on my already overtaxed
patience. [Rushes into the house in great excitement followed
by Cyrus.]

ACT FIRST, SCENE FOURTH.

The inside of Sir Henry's room with background scenery.

Enter Sir Henry after the assassination of Admr. in the
backgrounds.

Sir Hen. [Solus]—[wringing his hands in despair] What! is it
possible that I must plunge deeper into the mire? Is my soul
not now too much blackened with the charge of innocent blood?
Ah! cruel destiny! The tide moves to' and fro· and all the

mighty elements of nature seem to change at times, but he upon
whom fate lays his iron hand is at once the victim of the invinci-
ble and the slave of the incomprehensible. I have been inveigled
into the committal of this crime by some perfidious imp who now
foreshadows my utter ruin and who,' by his taunts, racks my
brains by night and disturbs my peace by day. Alas! perhaps
the solitude of the tomb will afford me some relief since every
earthly measure seems to have faded away. [walks backward and
forward rapidly.]

Enter Cyrus through R. D.

Cy.—[excitedly.] – A terrible murder has just been perpretrated, over which there hangs a profound mystery. I expect a gen ·
eral uproar in the village as soon as the fact becemes generally
known.

Sir Henry.—In what district was this murder committed ?

Cy.—Just over yonder, within the limits of this Barony.

Sir Henry.—[quickly,]—Upon whom does suspicion rest?

Cy.—Believing your tormentor to be the guilty person, and
fearing that any suspicion might rest upon yourself, with the ad-
mitted fact of his being with him last, I had the villian safely
incarcerated to await developments.

Sir Henry.—[confidently.]—Your intentions were, I know, always directed in my interest, for which good service I will intrust
to you the secret, but you must promise me eternal secresy.

Cy.—To you I do. ·

Sir Henry.—Fully confident of his having all the papers be·
longing to the estate, and under the impression that he meant to
do me all the evil he could, I had to resort to this extreme method
for my immediate protection. But upon searching deceased I

discovered that, true to his word, he had either misplaced or turned them over to the villian whom you have imprisoned. Now then my only hope is his removal, which I fear, will be the most difficult task of all.

Cy.—That is impossible. Had I done my best I could not have placed him in a safer spot.

Sir Henry.—Something must be done from this state of affairs. —[suddenly.]—To the goaler; demand the person of the intruder, take him to yonder woods, and there despatch him.

Cy.—[gloomily.]—Ah! But I fear I shall never get him from the goaler.

Sir.—Demand him in the name of the law. Take plenty of help with you and he will know no better; if it need be force, use it.

Cy.—I fear the feasability of such a project is too uncertain, ah, too uncertain.

Sir Henry.—What! am I to suffer a silent rebuke from the one to whom I have intrusted?—Does the one upon whom I have conferred every blessing, except life and light from Heaven at last find a flaw in my administration? Perhaps this signifies more than I understand.

Cy.—Permit me to assure you that on the contrary, you have my heart and hand at any moment; but under the present circumstances I regret my inability to comply with your present demand. It is useless for me to say I am always willing to obey your most trivial orders; you have every proof of that. But by insolently demanding him I might get what you little think of in your haste. I will get him by tact if I can. But everything else to my mind, is hopeless.

Sir Henry.—[emphatically,]—You may use stratagem, but by stratagem or no stratagem, the invidious wretch must be removed. To be lenient with him would encourage him and annihilate the zest that demands his immediate destruction. Then go; remember the injunction, for should you fail to carry it out, then Heavens above help us! But this is no time for repining. What we need is a lasting determination to place his vociferous soul in the clutches of his eternal enemy. "I do swear by all the Sacred hosts—

Cy.—Don't, don't charge your poor soul with that which it may may never be able to pay, I entreat you.

Sir Henry.—We must form a precipice, down which all his aspiring ambition must plunge; the timely casting of the net into which his unparelled audacity must enter is a matter, to me, of the gravest importance. And the work will admit of no delay, either. May the devil, with one hundred legions enter this department and take—

Cy.—You've said enough; your ordere will be, without scruple, executed; bring no more curses upon us. I've served you faithfully for this number of years, and that which sprang from a cold friendship to an ardent love will not forsake you now. No; I am your friend in this trial as in every other.

Sir Henry.—Thank, my hearty thanks; you have saved me more than gold; your friendship is worthy of the King himself.

Cy.—[placing his hands on his shoulders,]—If I fail you will forgive me? You know now my heart is with you.

Sir Henry.—For Heaven's sake don't say fail; that means death.

Exit Cyrus.

Sir Hen.—[Solus.]—[disdainfully.]—
Is the scepter'd monarch with all the plebeians to rule?
If so what care I for the pomp and lustre of
Mammon? It is sad to send two souls to perdition
I know, but to undo what has been done can I?
Ah! even the smiles of my lady seem base now in trouble,
But seek not repose, my soul, till you gain your worthy prize.
Rather would I be a vulture and give the wild beasts,   *gore*
Then even to share my estate with the minion of a minion.
But as the clouds of despair deepen about me I almost
Wish to discumber myself of this charge, but no,
Be it as I said ; let no compassionate land move,
Nor will the flame of passion cease till his doom is sealed.

ACT II.

SCENE FIRST.

The inside of the Gaoler's Cottage, with prison in the back.

Timothy O'Rouric.—Be'gorra, I've been gaoler for more than
one score ten year', and I must confess that I niver had such a
noice gintleman under the roof of this prison before. Bud, ah,
the rascal, he's come down a peg in the world. Sure he was once
tho pet of the village, but now, the low catiff, he's by his unman-
ageable temper, brot on himself the just vengence of Law. Be'
the back of me neck, I'd rather be the gaoler in his little cottage
with his little family and the ould woman to look after things
when I am— [going down in pocket.]

Old woman.—[with a sigh.]—When you're drunk.

Tim.—Phat? It's mesel' that will bate that ould woman if she don't stop abusin' her poor husband in this manner.

Old woman.—You bate me once, and that was the time you got me. No woman ever got bate so bad as I did in you. I could have married better if I had'nt met you.

Tim.— It's mesel' that has a heavy charge when I have you at my back.

Old woman.—Oc' quit your blaging. Phat's the charge against the prisoner.

Tim.—The same that ought to be against yonrsel'. You have your poor ould husband murthered.

Old woman.—Oc' now, phat is it Tim.

Tim.—Did I not till you it wus murder it is. He's goen' throug a course of lipigation wud Sir Henry Rollins over be'ant' there, and, to make sure work of it, he murdered the man that had all the documents.

Old woman—It's not lipagation. It's litegation or leneation or phat ever the divel they call it.

Tim,—Don't I tell you don't be contradicen' me like that again. I teached in the big college before I left home and was conceded the fiist prize for grammar and some philologist. Now I must submit to your contradicting me in this manner.[Exit Old woman in anger.]

Tim.—I'm like a bird out owa cage when that ould woman laves me. [Song by Tim.)

Enter Cyrus through L. D.

. Cy.—Gaoler, you look happy as lark this evening. But that is no wonder you are always happy. Have you still your prisoner?

Tim.—Yes sir, there he is behind the bars.

Cy.—My master in moment of mirth tenders you, through me, his hearty congratulation for the able manner in which you have kept control of this audacious character and cruel monster in the shape of man. He also says that it is safe to say before I take him from you that our envied gaoler is the happiest and best fel-'low that ever held the gaoleship in this village.

Tim.—And phare are you going to take him to?

Cy.—My instructions were to convey him to the seat of government and obtain a speedy trial, conviction, and punishment for a crime so odius to the peasantry of this shire that I fear the prison may be broken open at any moment and the prisoner taken out thereby defeating the ends of the law.

Tim.—(in deep meditation) Well–that–lukes–like–a–very .plausible- story if–I–was–sure- it– would--be-- right-- to--let--prisoner--go.

Sir Reu.—[who speaks from behind the prison door.]—Gaoler retain your charge to the last. He is but the instrument of an enemy who seeks my life. He has a number of men in yonder cut [pointing out] awaiting a signal from him to come and take me. If you deliver me up to him you are culpable for my death.

Cy.—You must not heed him. This is a matter of time with him. He is getting free lodging. I was also instructed to give you liberal compensation as a mark of his kind appreciation and for the further fulfilment of the duties that may be imposed upon you.

Tim.—Well, well, well. I've been gaoler for meny, meny years, and this is something I never saw yet, to send the gaoler money for holding the prisoner. Phy don't you git a written order from him so that I can convince everybody that I was acting under the instructions of my superior. [Gaoler turns around to his table and Cy. looks savagely at him.]

Cy.—Then having been gaoler for more than twenty-five years you never were fortunate enough to receive his good grace before? [Handing him the money.]

Tim.—Be me conscience, If I'd take that I could not rest to-no'it.

Cy.—[surprised,]—Then you reject the bounty of him to whom you owe your very existence? You miserable minion, stand aloft in bold defiance of a man who's power and wealth may be transmitted from land to sea? This man must submit to delay to satisfy your superstitious exactions? Mark you, should I be compelled to return for a written mandate you shall bring upon yourself the displeasure of his honor, with all the evils that may follow it.

Tim.—I only ax him to give me his word and honor on paper, that I've done my duty as far as I was able, and that he is responsible for the prisoner after he leave here. And awisha, that's not too much for him anyhow.

Cy.—[looking cautiously about him.]—Here, [pulliug out a bag of money,] you may have your price. Let me have prisoner and you need never be a gaoler any more. You can go to your native land and live sumptuously in the whole. You may have everything your heart may wish for. All this blessing I lay before you for the use of your keys.

Tim.—Faith it's not a blessing it wud be at all, at all, but a curse. Do you mean to entice me from the faithful discharge of my duties?

Cy.—[moving back,]—Understand me, it is not a bribe; I give

you this out of my own personal property to save me the delay my going back will cause.

Tim.—Yow must give me some security for the prisouer 'afore you can git him.

Cy.—Then to parcipitate the animosity between you, I must go through the desired formality, which you have just laid out for me. *

Tim.—Yes, so that I in the meantime may detarmine what course to pursue, as this is a case of more than ordinary interest to the denezens of our quaint little village. [Exit Cy. L. D., looking vengeance at Tim.] I could'nt depend much on me own jurisprudence, bud me humble opinion is that this is a clear case of bribery. Be gob, [bolting the door and closing the aperature through which the prisoner spoke,] I'll take special care of the prisoner for the future.

Enter Katie through R. D.

Katie.—[timidly]—Gaoler may I see your prisoner ?

Tim.—Oc' now, phat does a noice little girl like you want to see such a villian like that for? A pretty girl like you running after a murderer! Woulde'nt it do you to luke at mesel? [bracing up] Sure, and it's sorry I am, dear, that I can't accommodate you this time. But phat do you want wid him anyhow?

Katie.—[timidly]—My business is of such a nature as to permit me to confide it to him alone.

Tim.—Have you a lathur to give him? [putting his hand over his face.]

Katie.—No sir.

Tim.—[in an undertone,]—Is he your husband ?

Katie.—No sir.

Tim.—And phat in the name of since, do you want wid him?

Katie.—[fretfully,]—I would mnch rather impart this important information to himself. O please do let me converse with him one minute. Every moment you detain me hurrys him nearer and nearer to the hands of a voracious enemy whom I know to have laid plans for his murder.

Tim—.For his murder?   •

For his murder? O now, you mean for his removal from prison. Who could be at the bottom of this horrible maneuver?

Katie.—Will you protect me should they discover the object of my errand here to-night?

Tim.—Be the hokey smokey I will as long as I am able to stand up. All I want is a chance to die for some noice girl.

Katie.—(cautiously, looking around,) Then should Cyrus Old-burn, with a number of men, come to-night, and, under the cloak of authority, demand your prisoner, you may be sure that he is bent on the work of his ruin. So I entreat you, under these distressing circumstances, to use every and all means in your power to defeat him in the base scheme which they have just devised to take the life of an innocent man. But [in an undertone] such wealth and influence are invaribly destined to supass the harmless endeavors of the poor gaoler. May I again ask your permission to see him? I fear you won't be successful in your attempt to hold him, and my most anxious desire is to see him once more. Just please give me this one opportunity to converse with him.

(A noise is heard from the outside.)

Katie.—(suddenly,) —O gracious! there he is now. I must fly for my life.

(Exit Katie through r. d.)

Tim.—Let her story be true or uutrue, I must hold the prisoner. My only hope now is to depend on the volunteers. One tap
of the tower bell will bring me all the assistance I nade. (taps
the bell. Enter villagers.)

Vill.—What's—what's the matter?

Tim.—Now, stand out in the coroder and await my signal.

Enter Cyrus through L. D.

Cy.—(unsuspectingly,)—What are those men loitering about
the corridors for?

Tim.—Them men are there to aid the gaoler in tne execution
of his duties and for the preservation of law and order.

Cy.—Very good, sustain the cause of right and justice, and, as
you have gained favor with my master you will gain the respect
and admiration of the entire populace. Here (pulling a paper
from his breast,) is the note that his Honor sent you. I anticipat-
ed his bitter denunciation of you for your misconduct, but, to my
surprise he smilingly tells me that he highly commends your con-
stancy. That he attributes it to the practical manner in which
you are compelled to deal with your boisterous prisoners. He
also tells me that a true spirit of patriotism always outlines your
every action, which is more sublime in you, a foreigner, and in
your humble station in life than it would be in the crowned heads
of Monarchs, who Kingdom in nearly every case is their all. $8

Tim.—[holding the note up,]—Phat dus that say? I can't
start it. If I could start it I'd be all right.

Cy.—Perhaps you don't understand it. [Taking it from him.]
It's contents are as follows: Gaoler, I heartily commend your
stability in performing what you deem to be your duty, but upon
presentation of :his note, deliver up, forthwith, all right and

authority to retain the prisoner any longer. Now sir, you have the honor of detaining him for want of formality, an act few but yourself, under similar circumstances, could safely attempt.

Tim.—Give me the lathur till I see yeu again.

Cy.—[with petulence,]—You don't need it. I did this only for formality sake, and to teach others to respect your authority.

Tim.—[emphatically]—Now I am convinced that your business is dark and your pretended authority void. Before I would'ent give you the prisoner without an order, now I'm determined, by the support of these citizens who stand outside in the coroders in readiness for my signal, to hold the prisoner at the imminent risk of my life.

Cy.—[in a rage,]—What, sir, do you still persist in your preverse ways, notwithstanding the commands and entreaties of your superior? Do you mean to arrogate supremacy, or what may I infer from this inexplainable conduct? Do you not acknowledge the validity of his commanding you to obey him, or has your stupendous ignorance so blinded you as to render you senseless altogether? There will be no more formality used to humor you in your astounding grasp for legal authority. Well, I must say you are a highly qualified object for a kingdom. Your very appearance bespeaks an abundance of nothingness with little or no aspiration for even ordinary civilization. Under these circumstances the purple robe and diadem would handsomely become such a direful insignificance.

Tim.—[sharply]—Be the bulk owa tub I'm now the Monarch of meown house, and not a slave to the opinions of any man. I know the poor ould gaoler may take to his heels as soon as an oppertunity presents its'sel', bud sure I'd rather sacrifice my position than me conscience ony time. I'd be afeard the divil 'ud gallup off wud me before morning' if I'd do that.

Cy.—[aside in an undertone,]—'Who the devil could have informed this incorruptible idiot of my design? [aloud] I have been empowered by a man of authority to obtain the prisoner at any hazard, and, in obedience to him, you must deliver him up. I will not be detered by an an indolent, stupid fellow who knows not the moment his senses will leave him. It now becomes evident that I must impart to you the fact that for your contumacious action I could, in as much time as it takes to tell you, call in the soldiers and take possession of yourself and prisoner together

Tim.—[emphatically]—It's yoursel' that ought to be in prison instead of me. The ould woman has enough to do wid out attendn' to my duties phen her poor ould husband is in prison.

Cy.—Am I to hear you say again, as emphatic as ever, that, regardless of my commission, you do hold and will maintain the right to hold the prisoner?

Tim.—Yes, you think ould Tim's stupid, bud he knows that lather is no use to him widu' a name to it. Sure and they 'udent know bud it cum from the old divil himsel'.

Cy.—When I positively declare that this letter is from Sir Henry Rollins to you, do you boldly and in addition to the numerous indignities already offered, openly doubt my veracity?

Tim.—Yes; the lathur may be from him, bud he either forgot to put his name to it, or you,' to save your thrip back, made it yoursel'.

Cy.—The exigencies of this case will permit of no more delay. So come now, give me the object of my errand.

Tim.—[with a sneer,]—Nivir, sir, on a reccommendation like that.

Cy,—[in anger,]— Curse your odious jibes, I have put forth every and all the reason at my command to quiet your conscience, as I thought that was the trouble, but no, you still defy me. [He takes, by force, the keys which hang by Tim's side, but before he has time to open the door, the bell is tapped, to which the volunteers rush in, and Cyrus out through l. d.]

Tim.—Pursue him, pursue the villian, I am kilt from him! [Making wild gestures] It's mesel' that bate that gintleman owa I wanted too.

ACT SECOND, SCENE SECOND.

A romantic spot within a small wood, a willow tree overhanging a deep and rocky ravine, through which a torrent flows from the background, in front and under is a tree, a table and papers, at which are seated Lord Allison and a number of vassal Knights.

Enter Sir Henry Rollins and Cyrus Oldburn thro' L. D.

Lord Allison.—Welcome, my happy friend, welcome! [rising from his seat to greet them.] Your grasp seems cold; your countenance dismal.

Sir Henry Rollins.—Be assured, my Lord your courtesy is heartily received. If I could but express my innermost thoughts as they rest within my bosom you would fully comprehend how lasting the friendship I bear thee.

Lord Allison.—Though something strange has overcome you I know your sentiments are good. [To guards.] Bring forth your prisoner.

[Enter prisoner, with a guard on each side of him.]

Lord Allison—Prisoner come forward. It has been ordained for many of the ages of this world, that life should be taken for life, eye for eye, tooth for tooth. Hence in the name of his supreme Majesty and in pursuance of this decree, we will use our utmost efforts to fathom out this mystery and mete out the guilty the just penalty for his transgression of the law. [The deposition is next read] In accord to with the fact testified, to that on the Western borders of Henry Rollin's Park close by the torrent the mangled and bleeding form of Quartus Mathen, our most worthy citzen, has been found showing evidence of a dark murder. [To prisoner] The supposed cause of your having committed this terrible crime is that on the eve of your intended plunder in order that you might abrogate your voluntary promise to equal shares, you came to a pretended disagreement with the aforsaid appalling result.

Cy.—My Lord, besides this it is said, he acted in prison as though the enormity of his crime so preyed upon his mind as to bring on spasmodic convulsions in which he confessed his guilt and begged pitifully for the mercy of the Court.

Lord Allison—His strange attire on the evening of the murder is now explained.

Cy.—Yes, and that is not all, my Lord his anxious inquiries while in prison about the feeling of the peasantry towards him, with his numerous confessions in his moments of despondency leaves not the possibility of a doubt as to who is guilty.

Sir Hen.—My Lord, chancing to be on my battlements at the time of this unfortunate occurrence, and attracted by the cries of the victim, I saw the flight of a man whom upon close observation I recognized to be our culprit.

Lord Allison—Then from the view you had of the surrounding hamlets, you could very easily have seen him in the act.

Sir Hen.—My Lord the extreme darkness of the wood with the sombre shadows of a September's evening alone prevented my seeing him commit the deed, though I doubt not his being the man.

Cy.—I am told My Lord his every word and action, since the crime became publicly known, betrays that of a guilty conscience and a branded villain. I have myself been watching for a fortnight or more, his loitering about the parks as though he was bent on some diabolical work unknown to everybody save himself.

Lord Allison—[to prisoner] What are we to hear from you in reply to these prepared charges? Can you remain unmoved to all this? Know you not your life is in jeopardy for this brutal crime?

Sir Reu.—Should I speak I would protest my innocence, and that would be useless on the face of such heartless falsehood as I have just heard.

Cy.—My Lord durst he so speak in your presence?

Sir Hen.—[cooly.] My Lord he trys hard to excite your sympathy.

Cy.—His inverse method (which he frequently makes to accomplish an object) has been a scource of constant uproar in this village since the moment he betook himself within its boundery.

Lord Allison—[gravely] Sorry bairn no doubt the bright future laid out by your hopeful parents, has been sadly prolific of but one series of unmasked detentions In what locality were you on the evening of this terrible murder?

Sir Reu —My Lord if it occurred under the shadows of night, I was wrapp't in the seclusions of my bed chamber.

Lord Allison—Under whose roof have you sheltered since you have, as you say "resumed the old standard?" And who is likely to know the most about you?

Sir Reu.—The prison roof has been my shelter for more than half the entire period of time that I have been here My Lord, though anybody in the village upon a second thought should know me.

Lord Allison—[to Sir Henry] We can perhaps get some interesting facts from the gaoler.

Sir Hen.—[very nervously] No My Lord his most anxious desire is that you should send for a man whom he knows, by a series of delusions and unsurpassable promises, he can get to aver anything. Your simplicity of the low class shocks me. ✦

Cy.—[angrily but suddenly taken back] I protest, this man is so obtuse in his intellect that to employ his attention for an instant would be but a relapse of time.

Lord Allison—However, it is extremely essential that we should afford him every opportunity possible to establish his innocence. I am very favorably impressed with his demeanor throughout the entire proceedings.

Sir Hen.—[more nervous than before] But, My Lord, these tricks are his sole reliance. He knows his only hope is in all characters of this stamp he can get.

Cy.—[very nervously] My Lord, pray send for a man with at least ordinary endowments.

42

Lord Allison—If you have any particular antipathy to his coming he my remain.

Cy.—[serenely] No, My Lord, only to save you the displeasure of his repulsive dialect.

Lord Allison—I appreciate your kindness. And you Sir, Henry Rollins, a keen conception of my feeling and interest, has has always been a noteworthy feature in your career. But [aside to Henry] we should give him a hearing at any hazard. The circumstances involved in this case are of a very serious nature, from the fact that the life of an innocent or guilty man depends upon it. [to guards] Go deliver this to gaoler. [to prisoner] Your former associates and their characters don't accord well with good raising. It in itself bears sufficient testimony to condemn you.

Sir Reu.—[timidly] So be it My Lord; the truthful future will develope the secret.

Lord Allison [gravely] Ah! I fear the future will be too slow, for you, to bear the desired information, yes too slow. (Enter Tim through r. d.) (To Tim.) What was the conduct of the prisoner during the time he was under your charge?

Tim.—Ah the rascal! Well I must say though, he acted like a big Lord ever since he came under my roof.

Lord Allison—(aside to Sir Heny) Is it possible he is so utterly void of understanding as this? [To Tim] You say as unfeigned as before that he entrusted to you no secrets?

Tim.—Faith, I do your honor. The main villain denied every-thing I'd ask him to the last.

Cy.—My Lord he is suffering from a contusion which he received while in a state of intoxication.

Lord Allison.—Did he not, assisted by his friends, attempt to break forth from the prison?

Tim.—No your Honor, but I had a divil of a time to hould him. This gentleman (pointing to Cyrus) cum' last night and offered me some money to give him charge of my keys and I had to call the near peasauts to help me. (Consternation.)

Sir Henry—(with slight anger) It is just as I tell you MY Lord, he is altogether unreliable from the fact that any assertion he makes is directed in the interest of his friend.

Tim.—Faith and it's Katie that could tell you more about it than mesel.

Lord Allison—(very much agitated.) Who? What Katie? (as if awakening to an understanding) This is astounding.

Tim.—The little miss that lives under the same roof with himsel.

Sir Hen.—(more nervously than before) My Lord his impenetrable ignorance shocks my whole nervous sytem. I would exhort your Honor to bring the proceedings to a speedy sequel, as you see this information will avail us nothing.

Lord Allison—(To Tim.) Your testimony only tends to confuse me. My convictions are that your ill use of the crurskin has left you void of pour senses.

Tim.—It's mistaken you are if you think I'm crazy. Do you think would I be fursayen anything fur the base murderer? If his gude parents knowed what a sad end he cum to, it's little theyed rest now.

Lord Allison—What do you know about his parents? He is said to be an entire stranger here in the village.

Tim.—(timidly) No your Honor but on the contrary everyone

i n the village knaws him. It's mesel knawed when he was a better lad.

Lord Allison—(To prisoner) Prisoner relieve your concience of a repulsive burden by openly confessing your guilt of the hidious crime and the debasing passion that prevailed upon your better rerson to concede to it. I must now pronounce the fatal words that will forever sever your connection with anything mortal.

Sir Reu.—[with feeling] My Lord should the ghastly spectacle of his mangled form stand here now in the dread silence of death in readiness to confute any untruth, from me, I now solemnly declare before him who knows the secrets of hearts, to you, and before him the victim of some cruel wretch, that I am innocent.

Enter Kate through L. D.

Tim.—Now Katie. you touldt me—

Cy.—Hush, hush [catches him by the collar and shoves him back] retire you are needed no longer.

Lord Allison—[Katie comes in takes left side of Sir Reuben] The gaoler imparts to us the startling information that you know the villain who murdered the late Quartus Mathen. Did the prisoner ever entrust to you the secret of his guilt?

Katie—[timidly] No, your Honor he made no confession to me

Lord Allison—(emphatically) Do you know the perpretrator? [Sir Henry walks to and fro showing great emotion.]

Cy.—Now My Lord you need no assuring words to prove the venialty of this girl; it's conspicuous to even our most intolerable adversary. She knows he is the base scoundrel that perpretrated the murder and takes silence as a weapon to defend him.

Lord Allison—[To Katie] The mystery becomes deeper

and deeper every moment. Are you still reluctant? Then you confirm his assertion by still maintaining your peace. [arising) Prisoner your complacency is commendable, but from the power of the evidence received I must—

Katie—[suddenly] O no [catching his arm] My Lord, there is the man [pointing to Sir Henry] there is the perpretator and there is his accomplice[pointing to Cyrus. Surprise and confusion all around.]

Sir Henry in extreme despondency stammers "Who? What?" Then drawing his sword he plunges it into his bosom but before he falls he utters these words "O delusions upon delusions that brought here and thus blasted forever my fondest hopes." Then sinking to the floor.

Cy.—[suddeniy recovering. To prisoner] Ah! your insatiable malice has at last found an aperture through which to work out your venemous designs. And you [rushing at Katie.]

Sir Reu.—[pushing him back] Stop in time to save repentance. For though I have borne you as a masterpiece of deception, you may yet bring upon yourself that which charity alone has denied you. Your friend and you belong to the same school.

Cy.—[angrily. To Sir Reuben] Your future is framed; your fortune is amassed and may they be your ruin. May the fruits of your ill-gotten gains bring desolation upon you and your whole posterity. O that you who caused his downfall, ever stand aghast before the relentless gnawing of everlasting flame. [turning to Sir Henry who lies on in the same position.] Thus do's as noble a soul as ever animated a human frame, fall miserably to the earth in despondency and ignomy at the becon of a begrimmed beggar. Alas! a woman's perfidy, insolence and utter ignorance seem to have conquered the mighty Knight. Sure his faults were great, but his heart and hands were always open to the wants of the needy. Yes were they, every grateful denizen to shed one tear in remembrace of the many blesssings extended, we would now one all weep tears of bitter sorrow. Would to Heaven that I could cast my lot with his. For, if as it is said, (that charity covers an abyss of sin,) he sleeps to-night gloriously and triumphantly amid the glistening stars with Him of legions forever and ever.